CW00850558

A FANFARE OF MUSICAL LIMERICKS

by Ron Rubin

To Dick,
With fond memories:

— Ron

Aug.

HAMPSTEAD
PRESS

Published by Hampstead Press
16 Heathville Road,
N19 3AJ,
London,
United Kingdom
hampsteadpress @ blueyonder.co.uk

Text copyright © Ron Rubin

First published in 1986,
this revised and expanded edition published 2008.

ISBN 978-0-9557628-1-9

Illustrations and photographs are reproduced courtesy of the following
copyright holders: Hazeldine and Tim Holder

Layout, cover design and production by Marta Rusin

Printed and bound by Drukarnia GS, Cracow, Poland

A FANFARE OF MUSICAL LIMERICKS

by Ron Rubin

Illustrations:
Hazeldine
and Tim Holder

Foreword: Humphrey Lyttelton

'09

HAMPSTEAD
PRESS

Foreword by Humphrey Lyttelton

It has been often said that musicians have a style
of humour all to themselves. I am probably too close
to the trees to be able to define this particular wood,
but it's safe to say that 'musicians' humour' is born
in tribulation. No circumstance is too extreme for its
flowering, as exemplified by the story of the great tenor
saxist Zoot Sims, on his hospital death-bed, looking up
at the young doctor who was solemnly studying his
temperature chart and saying 'Say, doc, you're looking
a lot better today!'
Short of this, there are plenty of situations — on
interminable coach journeys, in slum band-rooms,
during soul-destroying residencies — when the choice
is a stark one between laughter and suicide. There
are several musicians who have done more than their
share of alleviating the darker hours with original
wit, and Ron Rubin is foremost amongst them. Any
musician will tell you that his limericks are no
haphazard exercises in doggerel, but encapsulate

profound truths. Though he is known to me under another name, I have worked many times with the trombonist Herb '...whose playing, though loud, was superb; when neighbours complained, young Herbert explained 'But great art is *meant* to disturb!"

I can think of one or two spots on the current touring circuit which still elicit from hardened campaigners the distressed comment of the drunken old drummer from Devon, who expired and ascended to heaven – but he cried 'This is Hades! There are no naughty ladies, and the pubs are all shut by eleven!' And nothing sums up more succinctly the dilemma of the jazz musician, peddling art in a commercialised world, than the fate of the bandleader of Lahore who played every darn tune in five-four – the other musicians quite liked these renditions but (wouldn't you know it?) the dancers all found it a bore.

If you still want a definition of 'musicians' humour', then read on. It's all there in Ron Rubin's wry observation and Tim Holder's dashing illustrations.

Ron Rubin

¶ And it came to pass in the days of Queen Victoria, that a man came forth out of the land of Russia unto the city of the Scousemen, yea, even unto Liverpool, and dwelt there. And he changed his name from Rubin Shereshevski to Shereshevski Rubin, because some comedian there told him it sounded more English. And he begat sons and grandsons, one of whom was called Ron, which is the whole point of this exercise.

¶ And Ron waxed older and went to Liverpool College and to Law School where he was exceedingly slothful, and far too interested in playing jazz musick and generally larking about. And his teachers were wroth with him, and there was a fair amount of gnashing of teeth. Wherefore Ron arose and shook the dust of that city from off his feet, and became a soldier in the army of the King. And when the prodigal returned, he ministered under his father as Chief Scribe for six summers. Then, one day, behold, a Voice called unto him, saying: Hearken! get thine finger out, Ron, and henceforth follow the True Path of jazz musick.

¶   Now in those days the Scousites walked after strange gods that their fathers knew not, and there was great tumult and twanging of guitars, so that all those with healthy earholes were sore astonished.

¶   Wherefore Ron girded up his loins and departed once more from the city of his fathers. And he dwelt in the South with his wife who was of the tribes of Ham and Japheth, yea, an Afro-Saxon woman. And they were fruitful and multiplied and begat four children. and to this day Ron playeth jazz musick upon the bass viol and the pianoforte. And thus saith he: Verily, this is a damn sight more fun than working.

There are few poetical forms that can boast the limerick's perfection. It has progression, development, variety, speed, climax and high mnemonic value. — CLIFTON FADIMAN

Part of the charm of the limerick is the surprise, the sudden swoop and unexpected twist of the last line.
— LOUIS UNTERMEYER

Essentially the limerick is an anecdote in verse.
— W.S. BARING-GOULD

LIMERICKS

The Piano

The piano's a clever invention,
But one thing perhaps I should mention:
    It's sensitive strings,
    Like the players — poor things —
Are always in need of attention.

The Double Bass

The bass is a thumping great brute,
And to play it's a thankless pursuit;
    The tail pin's so sharp, it
    Makes holes in your carpet —
Forget it and take up the flute!

The Conductor

Conductors, though quite ornamental,
Do tend to be too temperamental;
When it's time to rehearse,
They frequently curse,
And say things that no well-bred gent'll.

The Accordion
It's played by both ladies and fellows,
Who lustily heave at its bellows;
    It evokes Gay Paree,
    Country dancing, the sea,
And wild Buenos Aires bordellos.

The Alphorn
The alphorn holds little allure
For musicians; the reason I'm sure,
    Is the tone — so bizarre,
    And there's no repertoire —
And you can't get it through a swing door.

The Arranger

Arranging can be quite a chore,
But arrangers get crumpet galore;
    (Well, is it so strange?
    —After all, to arrange,
You've first got to learn how to score…)

The Bagpipes

When they set off to clobber their foes,
Those pipes make the Celts bellicose;
    (Me, too — that mad skirl
    Often tempts me to hurl
Something hard at the piper, God knows!)

The Cello

The type who would take up the cello
Is doubtless a sensitive fellow,
And much more refined
Than the brass, who're inclined
To be boozers who banter and bellow.

The Balalaika

With triangular shape most bizarre,
It's known as the Russian guitar;
    To the Russki, its twang
    Brings as poignant a pang
As vodka or choice caviare.

The Banjo

The banjo's implacable clank
Is not to my taste, to be frank;
    But it's loved by jazz traddies,
    And lasses and laddies
With names like Zeke, Tammy and Hank.

The Bassoon
A kind of bass oboe — but, my!
The players are touchy — just try
    To call the bassoon
    'The orchestral buffoon' —
You'll be asking for one in the eye!

The Cor Anglais
English it ain't, and what's more,
It's a woodwind, and no way a 'cor' —
    Which in French is a horn,
    But to those London-born,
Means (pardon my French…) *zut alors*!

The Drums

Some drummers get quite a big kick
From showing off every new trick;
   They love to hold 'clinics',
    Which prompts certain cynics
To ask: 'Are the blighters all sick?'

The Flute

It's handy, and takes up less space
Than the harp or the tuba or bass;
    It can chirrup and trill,
    But the *true* test of skill
Is maintaining that silly grimace.

The Glockenspiel

Like a distantly heard carousel,
It tinkles its magical spell...
(A word in your shell-like:
Its sound is quite bell-like —
A *glocke*, in fact, means a bell.)

The Guitar

A thing of both beauty and grace,
To hold it is like an embrace;
But sometimes, I fear,
What is meant for your ear
Can be rather too much in your face...

The Harp

It's hard to play harp, and no doubt,
Much harder to lug it about;
It's tuned to C-flat,
And the reason for that
Is to keep all the amateurs out.

The Mouth Organ

It won't cost you oodles of cash,
And it's easy to play — have a bash!
And so handy to carry —
You'll be happy as Larry,
Though minus, perhaps, his panache.

The Horn

Its sound is mellifluous, rich,
But it's truly quite tricky to pitch;
It evokes wooded places
And wide open spaces,
And is much used in cowboy-film kitsch.

.

The Clarinet
The hardest of woodwinds, perhaps;
The players, both ladies and chaps,
Need the nimblest of hands —
And some spare rubber bands,
As the metal bits tend to collapse.

CLARINAID
RUBBER BANDS

The Nose Flute

The nose flute's a curious thing,
And much favoured east of Nanking;
    But if you've congestion,
    It's out of the question,
And safer to whistle or sing.

The Piccolo

The piccolo looks like a toy,
And like toys, it is apt to annoy;
    Though maybe not quite as
    Acute as tinnitus,
Its twitter I do not enjoy.

The Recorder

It costs a lot less than a flute'll,
And its sound is quite sweet — never brutal;
So if you can afford a
Nice new recorder,
Go buy one and learn how to tootle!

The Saxophone

A hybrid that's misunderstood,
It's a woodwind that ain't made of wood;
Though the tenor's real hip,
The soprano — they quip
Is an ill wind that no one blows good…

The Oboe

Before the musicians can play,
The oboist signals an 'A',
    Thus staying immune
   From the charge: 'Out of tune!'
'It's you lot!' the player can say.

The Trombone

The trombone has a slide and a bell,
And a sound like a demon from hell;
It has seven positions —
Though many musicians
Know quite a few others as well...

The Trumpet

The trumpet's a heavenly thing,
Its fanfares are fit for a king;
    Gabriel blows one —
    Know why he chose one?
'You can't get those harps, man, to swing!'

The Tuba

The tuba is bulky, I know,
And it takes lots of effort to blow;
    If you're home's a bedsitter,
    Your wife could get bitter —
One of them may have to go…

Hazeldine

The Viola

The viola is somewhat akin
To the rather more glam violin;
But though some folk may sneer
At the players, it's clear
They can take it right there on the chin!

The Triangle

The triangle's easy to play,
You can master the thing in a day —
Or maybe a minute
(There's nothing much in it,
And nothing much more I can say.)

The Washboard

Skifflers it thrills and enthrals,
Though others it often appals;
But one thing's for sure —
When the band's out on tour,
It's handy for scrubbing your smalls.

The Xylophone
The xylophone makes much more din
Than the vibraphone, though they're akin;
    (They say some wild tribes
      Once exchanged theirs for vibes —
But where did they plug the things in?)

The Zither
It recalls that bad hat, Harry Lime,
Who ended his long life of crime
    In the sewers of Vienna,
      A grisly Gehenna
Of cascading waters and slime.

The Violin

The world loves a violin, of course;
But just think: that tone is perforce
                Produced by a cat
                When its lower anat.
Is scraped with the hair of a horse.

A talented chap from Bordeaux
Plays spoons in the clubs (semi-pro);
One night Uri Geller
Turned up in his cellar,
And cocked up the whole bloody show.

There was an old drummer of India,
Whose wife said:'Don't make such a din, dear!'
He demurred: 'Now look here,
I'm the best in Kashmir —
It's clear you have ears made of tin, dear!'

There was a young lady of Chester
Who idolized Victor Sylvester,
Till a jazz buff seduced her,
And soon introduced her
To Louis and Basie and Lester.

An ageing contralto from Leigh
Was as vain as a diva can be;
Though she tried hard to practice
The solfa, the fact is
She couldn't get further than 'ME'.

There was a young singer called Ida,
Whose mouth became wider and wider;
One dark winter's night,
A man with poor sight
Dropped several postcards inside her.

A gifted young lady called Amber
Has taken up viol de gamba;
    She's great on fandangos
    And bossas and tangos,
And as for her samba — Caramba!

A bluesman who went out to Italy
Reviewed his career somewhat bitterly:
    'Those cats out in Tuscany,'
    He said, 'just can't busk any —
But they do sing their folksongs quite prettily.'

A triangle player called Bart
Says: 'Please don't belittle my art -
        It took a whole week
        To reach this great peak,
And I play very much from the heart!'

A tenor who hailed from Lepanto
Was known for his splendid bel canto;
        But as for his *lieder*,
        His German, dear reader,
Was rather like bad Esperanto.

A drunken old drummer from Devon
Expired, and ascended to Heaven;
'But,' he cried, 'this is Hades!
There are no naughty ladies,
And the pubs are all shut by eleven!'

There was a young singer called Tess,
Who sang with more force than finesse;
When she reached for top C,
It sounded to me
Like the cry of a bird in distress.

There was a young fellow called Nobby,
Who played tenor sax for a hobby;
When he asked his wife Jane:
'Do I play like Coltrane?'
She said: 'Yes, dear — you sound just like
Robbie!'

Said an avant-garde jazzman called Jess,
When asked to explain his success:
     'I suppose it's my sound' —
     [Ed: Like cats being drowned]
'And technique' — [Ed: Another fine
mess...]

There was a trombonist called Herb,
Whose playing, though loud, was superb;
     When neighbours complained,
     Young Herbert explained:
'But great art is *meant* to disturb!'

There was a stout diva of Dorset
Who couldn't unfasten her corset,
    So she called the police, who
    Said: 'We can't release you —
Perhaps a good locksmith could force it?'

An earnest banjoist called Higgs
Does only the traddiest gigs;
He lives on a diet
(For God's sake don't try it!)
Of brown ale and mouldy old figs.

There was an old Welshman called Morgan,
Who had a magnificent organ;
Said his wife: 'You are blessed
With what must be the best
Hammond organ in all of Glamorgan!'

There was an old agent called Roscoe,
Who sent a Scots pipe band to Moscow;
But the Russians' reaction
Was mild stupefaction —
So next time he let old Joe Loss go.

A bandleader out in Lahore
Played every darned tune in five-four;
The other musicians
Quite liked these renditions,
But the dancers all found it a bore.

There was a trombonist called Grange,
Who had an incredible range:
Schoolgirls, stenographers,
Nuns, choreographers,
And sometimes boy scouts for a change.

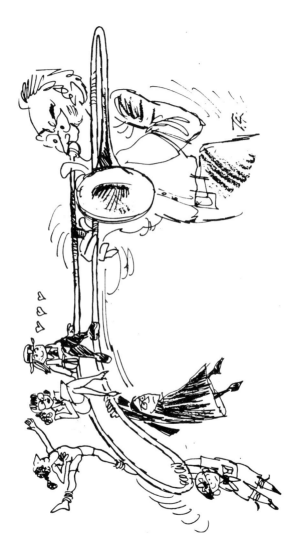

A pygmy once purchased a drumkit,
But found that he just couldn't hump it;
    And his arms were too short
    For trombone, so he bought
A cute little pocket-sized trumpet.

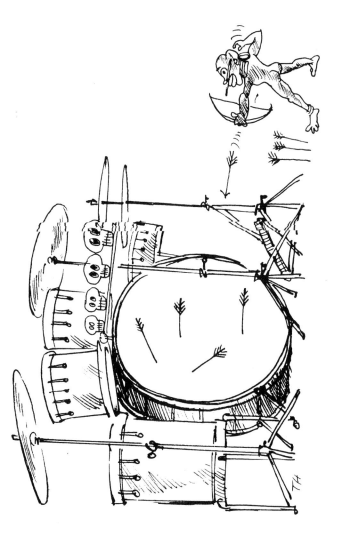

An accordion player called Lunt
Liked to play with his hands back to front;
This caused some dismay
Amongst the *au fait*,
But the crowd shouted: 'Wow — what a stunt!'

Says world-famous Ludwig van B.:
'I've written in every damn key;
But now that I'm deaf,
E minor or F?
— It's much of a muchness to me.'

A hermit who lived in Tibet
Was a dab hand at bass clarinet;
    He once taught a yak
    To play *Hit the Road, Jack!*
And selections from *No, No, Nanette.*

Auditioning, lovely Miss Bentley
Sang music-hall songs sentimentally;
    Said the agent: 'My dear,
    It's quite clear you've no ear —
And you haven't a voice, incidentally.'

Having dined rather well at the Hilton,
A contrabassoonist called Milton
Forked out fifty smackers
Then threw up cream crackers
And Stilton all over the Wilton.

A public house pianist of Dagenham
Played Chopin études — but liked raggin' 'em;
With his foot he played drum,
Whilst finger and thumb
Would dance down the keys with a fag in 'em.

An opera lover called Healey
Once put on *The Ring* in Swahili;
The natives of Hull
Found it all rather dull,
As did the good burghers of Ely.

There was a boy singer called Chad,
Whose voice started breaking: 'How sad,'
    Said his agent — 'it's clear
    That to save your career,
The answer's castration, my lad!'

A double bass player from Guelph
Grew old, and was left on the shelf;
    Said his leader: 'Dear friend,
    This isn't the end —
You're quite free to play with yourself!'

A young Aussie singer called Hilda
Adored singing *Waltzing Matilda*;
    For weeks, loud and shrill,
    She warbled until
An irate Aborigine killed her.

One night at a wild Irish ceilidh,
A visting Yank called Bill Beilidh
        Cried: 'Gee, what a band!
        It's so goddam bland —
I'm glad I grew up on Bill Heilidh!'

A duff old trombonist called Holt
Made even strong maestros revolt;
        He drove Barbirolli
        Clean off his trolley,
And once made Sir Adrian bolt.

'Bach,' says a pundit called Henty,
'Is revered by the world's cognoscenti;
    They all want to know
    Bach's Organ Works, so
I remind them — his brood numbered twenty.'

A pianist working in Reims
Would boast he knew thousands of themes,
    So when some young chap
    Shouted: 'Play me some Rap!'
He played *Wrap Your Troubles In Dreams*.

Music may be diatonic,
Chromatic or dodecaphonic;
        But how do we gauge
        The works of John Cage?
Come, come, let's be kind — cacophonic…

An amateur fiddler called Brad
Once bought what he thought was a Strad;
Said his wife: 'Look, my dear,
It says "Made in Korea" —
Too bad, Brad — I think you've been had!'

Though some might like music that's canned,
Most would prefer a live band;
Well, last night in Hayes,
We had it both ways —
A live band, all quite canned, on the stand.

A versatile lady of Epping
Does sessions, and all kinds of depping;
Her flute and her zither
She always takes with her,
But drumkits she doesn't like shlepping.

'Do you know,' asked a chappie called Dai,
'*I'm in Love with a Wonderful Guy*?'
The pianist replied,
Without losing his stride:
'I suppose, ducks, then this is goodbye?'

On piano, an old soak called Alan
One night drank much more than a gallon;
What was quite unforeseen,
When the band played *The Queen* —
Alan stood up and puked in the Challen.

A bebop trombonist called Clyde
Was a bit of a Jekyll and Hyde;
Near-normal by day,
At night he'd waylay
Punk-rockers with poison-tipped slide.

There was an old jazzman called Wood,
Whose playing was no bloody good;
    He idolized Louis,
      But his *Cornet Chop Suey*
Was much more like 'Trumpet Rice Pud'.

A hard-drinking mezzo soprano
Got stoned at La Scala, Milano;
    As they dragged her outside,
      'To hell with,' she cried,
Mens sana in corpore sano!'

A famous conductor from Calais
Was asked, whilst conducting the Hallé:
        'Can you play *Night and Day* ?'
        He replied: '*S'il vous plaît* —
Zis isn't ze 'Ammersmith Palais!'

When sober I love Debussy
And Mozart and Ludwig van B.,
        But when I am pissed,
        I prefer Brahms and Liszt —
Can someone explain this to me?

Some people play piano by ear,
For just a few quid and some beer;
But dear cousin Rose
Plays entirely by nose,
And makes twenty thousand a year.

There was a young man of Cape Cod,
Who thought Cecil Taylor was God;
So he practised for years,
But no one with ears
Would give him a gig — silly sod!

A scale may begin, as we know,
From any degree, high or low;
But there's one golden rule,
Which you don't learn at school —
Union Scale starts with DOUGH!

A Jewish violinist called Schott
Wears a skull-cap onstage: it is not,
He insists out of piety —
It's simply anxiety
That no one should see his bald spot.

'Mick Jagger's been knighted, I see,'
I said to my wife — 'Glory be!'
'Having listened, my dear,
To his music, it's clear
He's already benighted!' said she.

A guitarist who hails from Marbella
Was nagged by his wife: 'Juan, I tell ya —
You haven't used soap
Since Pius was Pope —
You smell like a rotten paella!'

An Athenian singer called Nina
Was partial, it seems, to Retsina;
    She's been all the rage
    Since she staggered on stage,
And stripped to a slow cavatina.

There was an old jazzman called Don
(And Heaven knows what he was on);
    His tombstone's inscribed:
    'For years he imbibed,
And now, folks, this cat's REALLY gone!'

A bandleader out in Caracas
Could never find agents or backers,
For although his big band
Looked incredibly grand,
They all played the same thing — maracas.

There was an old man of Hong Kong.
Who wrote a concerto for gong;
The critics adored it,
But some got quite bored (it
Was nine-and-a-half hours long…)

In concert, bassoonist Herr Keller
Sits near the trombones, poor old feller;
When things get too moist,
His habit's to hoist
A splendid, protective umbrella.

A trumpeter out in Managua
Would travel to sessions by jaguar;
The sort with four paws,
Not the sort with four doors —
Said his bandleader: 'Charles, what a wag
you are!'

There was an old flautist called Lessing,
Whose style was most unprepossessing;
     Said a critic from Tees:
     'It's not just the keys,
But the listeners that Lessing's depressing.'

There was an old man of Cologne,
Who played a decrepit trombone;
     Encrusted in verdigris,
     One went through the third degree
On hearing its hideous tone.

My grandpa plays bass and euphonium,
My grandma plays horn and harmonium;
      My father plays flute
      And my mother plays lute —
The result is complete pandemonium.

There was a young girl called Felicity,
Who had quite a flair for publicity;
      She'd play a Bach fugue
      On the synth or the Moog:
'To hell with,' she said, 'authenticity!'

A young keyboard player called Rigg
Says: 'The Yamaha's just what I dig —
　　　　It's such a delight
　　　　To play it all night
Then ride it back home from the gig!'

Says Freddie, a flautist from Bute:
'This object is known as a flute;
　　　Though some think it ought
　　　　To be renamed a 'flaut',
We flutists just don't give a hoot!'

Said the wife of dear old Rabbi Stern:
'As a cleric, it's peanuts you earn;
　　　Though the congregants go for
　　　　The sound of the shofar,
Trumpet it's better you learn!'

A guitarist by name of Renato
Made love somewhat *tempo rubato*;
    'At the rate that you strum,
    Said his girl, 'I won't come! —
Perhaps you should use some vibrato?'

A keen jazz musician called Mallory
Once asked for an increase in salary;
    Said the Guv'nor: 'No way!
    Till you buck up and play
Less bebop, and more to the gallery!'

There was an old drummer called Biggs,
Who kept a baboon in his digs;
He taught it *Take Five*,
And how to talk jive,
And it carried his drumkit to gigs.

A young piano student called Hughes,
Who was booked for a round-the-world cruise,
        Played nothing but Czerny
        Throughout the long journey,
Which drove half the punters to booze.

An ageing violinist from Italy
Considered his pate somewhat bitterly:
        'It's almost as neat as
        The dome of St Peter's,
But not rounded off quite so prettily.'

'Grand Opera,' says dear Auntie Bess,
'Is not to my taste, I confess;
    Though it's all so spectacular,
        I prefer the vernacular -
Just give me old Gilbert and S!'

A talented harpist, Miss Butler
(Whose playing could not have been subtler)
        Once worked on a ship
        But regretted the trip
When the Captain decided to scuttle her.
(The ship, that is, not Miss Butler...)

Said Handel: 'Please don't call me Herr —
I'm really quite British — so there!
And please, ven I croak,
I vould like (vot a joke!)
A coffin marked: 'Handel With Care''!'

Said the leader to vocalist Pat;
'We're way into overtime — drat!
　　　How fast d'you suppose
　　　You can sing *Vie En Rose* ?'
Well, she did it in one minute — flat.

A famous soprano, Miss Strong,
Had a nose that was nine inches long;
　　　At La Scala, Milano,
　　　They dubbed her 'Soprano
De Bergerac, Empress of Song'.

The clarinet's sound is unique,
And the player needs bags of technique:
So please do not gloat
When that poignant high note
Turns into a hideous squeak.

There was a young cat from Carlisle,
Who only played once in a while;
He made little bread,
For, as I just said,
He only played *Once In A While*...

An osteopath, name of Maxwell,
Is an expert at making folk's backs well;
His greatest ambition
Is to be a musician
But no one thinks Maxwell plays sax well.

Says a triangle player called Nat
(Who's tone-deaf, and a bit of a prat):
       'It's great fun to play,
       And who's there to say
If I'm playing the thing sharp or flat?'

Said a punter to bandleader Ron:
'Do you think you could play *C'est Si Bon*?'
       'We *could*,' Ronnie hissed,
       'But as you're so pissed,
I think we'll play *After You've Gone*!'

Each Christmas, with kith and with kin,
We visit our old village inn,
Where the local brass band'll
As always, play Handel,
And Handel, as ever, will win.

An oddball musician from Lytham
Has just about no sense of rhythm;
He busks in the Strand
With his own one-man band,
For nobody else will play with him.

There was an old bass called d'Amato.
Who sang quite *appassionato*;
We all shed a tear
When he fell on his spear,
But he's now quite a well-known castrato.

A spoons virtuoso from Yorks
Gives erudite Arts Council talks;
He started on ladle
Whilst still in the cradle
And now even plays knives and forks.

Italians love Paganini,
Puccini and Signor Rossini;
But lately I've found
They're more thrilled by the sound
Of an expertly-tuned Lamborghini.

There was a young diva called Pru,
Who had an affair with a gnu;
      To meddle with gnus
      Is surely bad news,
But Pru says: *'Chacun à son goût!'*

An elderly bassist called Gus
Was humping his gear to a bus,
      But the amp was so weighty
      (And Gus nearly eighty)
Now the poor bugger's wearing a truss.

A New Music critic called Roth
Was nipped on the ear by a moth;
But the moth's motivation
Was simply starvation
For Roth had two ears made of cloth.

A piccolo player called Armit
Who bought a pet snake, tried to charm it;
It couldn't resist
Count Basie and Liszt,
But Stockhausen seemed to alarm it.

There was an old jazzman called Randall,
Who listened to Mozart and Handel;
But Mozart and Handel
Had never heard Randall,
Which Randall thought rather a scandal.

'Good News!' said the Preacher, 'give ear -
The Messiah is due to appear!'
(Bad news, say the choir —
The blooming 'Messiah'
Comes year after year after year…)

A retired ballerina called Gwen
Took up her vocation again;
But her technique had gone,
And her famed 'dying swan'
Expired like a rather sick hen.

A lady who lived near Loch Ness
Was asked in a quiz: 'Can you guess
    The Queen's favourite tune?'
    She ventured: '*Blue Moon*?'
But the answer was 'Corgi and Bess'.

The gigster, or jobbing musician,
Works in places both pleb and patrician;
At knees-ups and marriages,
Or banquets at Claridge's,
He may ponder the human condition.

A weird piano player called Mose
Was blessed with extremely long toes;
Such was their length,
He could stretch a full tenth,
But only on ballads and slows.

There once was a great prima donna,
Whose co-star leaped madly upon her:
'Let's make it!' he cried;
'Sure thing,' she replied,
But right here on stage I don't wanna!'

An Eskimo in his igloo
Used to practise all day on kazoo;
His wife sang along
And their favourite song
Was *I Only Have Ice* [sic] *For You*.

An avant-garde jazzman from Tees
Liked to play with his elbows and knees;
When I growled: 'That's a fine way
To treat a good Steinway!'
He said: 'Shush, mate — I'm counting my fees!'

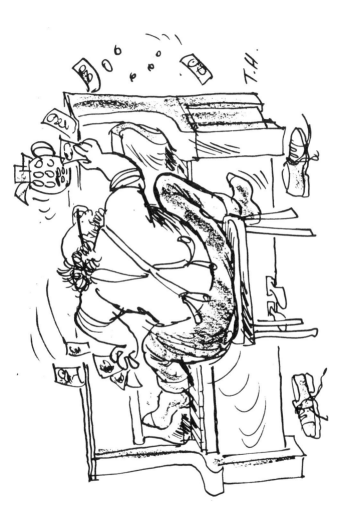

A sousaphone player called Garnett
Once behaved like the Devil incarnate,
When one rose-tinted dawn,
He puked down his horn
At an interesting gig up in Barnet.

A youngish trombonist called Campbell
(And that bit is just the preamble)
Having quaffed fourteen jars,
Played the first fifteen bars
Of what might have been *Didn't He
Ramble...*

On Verdi, Giuseppe, I'm keen;
His name — if you know what I mean —
    Quite rolls off the tongue,
    (It can almost be sung)
— A pity it just means Joe Green.

A trad band from Aix-la-Chapelle
Once went on a short tour of Hell;
    They played *When the Saints* —
    Not many complaints —
And met their old agent as well.

A lady guitarist of Bude
Was asked: 'Can you play *In The Mood* ?'
She replied: 'Why not — sure!'
But her hearing was poor,
And she stripped off and played in the nude.

A young rock 'n' roller from Tring
Was convinced his career would take wing,
But he never quite clicked,
For the public felt tricked
When they found out the fellow could sing.

When a dreadful brass band in Wood Green
Struck up with *Begin the Beguine*,
The people all stood
(As, by jingo, they should!)
For it sounded like *God Save the Queen*.

An opera singer called Mae
Sang *Carmen* in Haifa one day;
 The audience booed her
 And a critic reviewed her
In two little words, viz. 'Oy vey!'

When the opera came to Stoke Poges,
We plebs went and sat in the loges;
 But one singer from Italy
 Complained rather bitterly:
'Back home they're reserved for the doges.'

Too late it's becoming quite clear
That I don't have a musical ear;
Old Hamish says: 'Och,
You've an ear like Van Gogh —
Ye should have made art your career!'

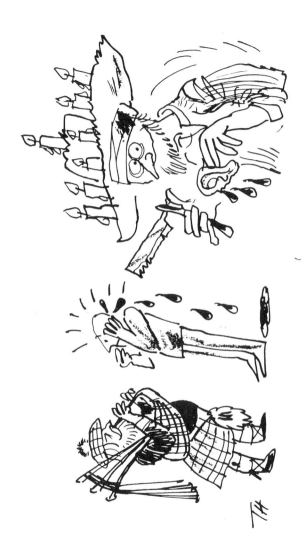

An O.A.P. out in Rangoon,
Who took up the contrabassoon,
Dropped dead, so they say,
Whilst attempting to play
An up-tempo *How High The Moon*.

There was an old man of Killarney,
Who loved Johnny Hodges and Carney;
This caused bitter strife
Between him and his wife,
For she simply adored Mantovani.

A boozy young student called Twist,
Used to dream he could play like Franz Liszt;
      He'd got the technique,
      But his will-power was weak,
And you can't play like Liszt when you're drunk.

An androgynous chappie called Peake
Had a range that was surely unique;
      He sang bass and contralto,
      Soprano and alto —
But his treble was more like a shriek.

Our club has a bouncer outside,
Who's seven feet tall, and as wide;
He's actually paid
To drum up some trade
By chucking the punters *inside*.

There was an old dustman called Max,
Who played jazz and blues to relax;
Though hopeless on drums,
And on piano all thumbs,
He was quite a dab hand on the sacks...

A castanets player of Wycombe
Loved to play — night and day he would
click 'em;
His neighbours went mad
Till one smart young lad
Was persuaded to break in and nick 'em.

A keen Wagner fan is our Geoff,
Especially when played *triple f;*
    'Some folk find him hellish,'
    Says Geoff, 'but I relish
The noise, as I'm almost stone deaf!'

A glockenspiel player called Rockwell
Did a gig at a rock club in Stockwell;
    Said the Guv'nor: 'The crowd
    Like their music real loud —
Get an amp, and we might hear the glock well!'

A gifted young cat from the Bronx
Plays horn in some wild honky-tonks;
Says his boss: 'It's a waste
To show any good taste —
Give'em plenty of growls, squeaks and honks!'

Said an elderly jazzman called Moore:
'My future looks dashed insecure;
I once was, of course,
A great *tour de force* —
Now, alas, I am just forced to tour!'

A student conductor called Russ
Would boast to his lady friends, thus:
　　'Mark my words — I'll go far!'
　　And he did — to Qatar,
Where I hear he's conducting a bus.

Says a freelance musician called Tate:
'I work for the Union rate;
　　But I do put my fees up
　　For playing a knees-up
Or music I thoroughly hate.'

There was an old Sikh of New Delhi,
Who modelled himself on George Melly;
He'd the voice and the smile
And sartorial style,
But he couldn't quite manage the belly.

A buxom young dancer called Cleo
Did cabaret way down in Rio;
    Each night when she rhumba'd,
    Her breasts, unencumbered
By corsage, would join in *con brio*.

Violin and viola, we learn,
Are different. But how to discern
Which is which? Well the latter
Is bigger and fatter —
And take a bit longer to burn...

A New Orleans jazzman called Price
Would thus give his pupils advice:
'Play stomps, rags and blues,
Drink gallons of booze,
And eat nothing but red beans and rice!'

Drummers — and drums — have thick skin,
But the bass player's pelt is quite thin;
So never enquire
(The results could be dire!)
'How d'you get that thing under your chin?'

A versatile lady called Lola
Plays harp, double bass and viola,
Banjo and bassoon,
All quite out of tune —
But she's great on the old pianola.

There was a young G.I. called Sherman,
(Who'd once played the flugel with
Herman);
　'You gotta play bugle!'
Said the bandmaster, 'flugel
Is out of the question — it's German!'

Says a bassist who hails from Nantucket:
'*Arco*?' — no, man — I just pluck it;
But I do have a bow,
Though it's only for show —
Look, I keep it right here in this bucket!'

To the choirmaster, chorister Darryl
Said: 'Yes, we enjoy the odd carol;
But we'd much rather sing
A song with some zing —
Like, how about *Roll Out The Barrel* ?'

'Our new French *chanteuse*,' grumbled Lars,
'Has a repertoire really too sparse,
And her pitching is poor —
But the band all adore
The way that the girl rolls her Rs!'

A young jazz musician called Potts
Was asked if he'd play Ronnie Scott's:
'I'd love to — and how!'
Said Potts, but right now
The band is all tied up in Notts.'

A roving musician called Rubin
Liked black coffee, with one sugar cube in;
But one night in Bombay,
At a topless café,
It was served to him white, with one boob in.

Says Godbolt, a crusty old gent:
'As agent, my life was misspent;'
But now as a writer,
The world seems much brighter,
Though he misses the old ten per cent...

A cloth-eared old cellist called Mitch
Was wed to an absolute bitch;
But he kept her, poor fellow,
To tune up his cello,
For the woman had absolute pitch.

The Blues is an art steeped in myth,
Its sounds full of pathos and pith;
    It's plucked with the fingers,
    Or shouted by singers,
Most of them ladies called Smith.

There was a young girl called Romola,
Who starved when she played the viola;
    Then she met a smart fellow,
    Who ran a bordello —
Now she's driving around in a Roller.

A madcup punk rocker called Bostock
Once played in East Germany (Rostock),
Where he smashed his guitar
On a large Commisar:
Now he's mining in far Vladivostock.

The piano has eighty-eight keys,
But much more important than these
Is the key to the lid,
Which (Heaven forbid!)
If you lose it — no gig and no fees!

There was a young jazzman called Chet,
Who launched a progressive octet;
Though the crits were ecstatic,
The end was traumatic,
And Chet is ten thousand in debt.

A colleague of mine has, unhappily,
Acquired his Italian scrappily;
    He thinks *pizzicato*
    Is made from tomato
And pasta, and eaten in Napoli.

A bagpiper busking in Cheltenham
Waylaid folk, and ran about beltin' 'em;
    When had up in court,
    He explained that a quart
Of the hard stuff just brought out the
    Celt in him.

There was a young fellow called Bradley,
Who did almost everything badly;
        He took up the uke,
      And played songs by Duke —
But nobody loved him too madly.

A quirky composer called Coote
Wrote pieces for viol and flute;
  The music for viol,
  Though vile, made a pile,
But the pieces for flute made no loot.

Says Sid, a fastidious Scouse:
'I dig all that music by Strauss —
  The one called Johann,
  But the other one, man,
I wouldn't let into me house!'

Said Fred to his wife: 'It's quite plain, dear —
The choirmaster's sozzled again, dear:
    That's not *The Messiah* —
    He's got the whole choir
Singing something to do with a reindeer…'

Our dancing instructor, old Titus,
Does steps which amaze and delight us;
    His leaps to the ceiling
    Are performed with great feeling —
They say that his muse is St Vitus.

There was an old crooner called Christie,
Who used to get terribly pissed, he
Would sing the same song
The whole damn night long,
(Which may or may not have been *Misty*...)

A zealous composer called Grace
Says: 'My musical goal's to embrace
    The whole range of strings —
    They're *such* lovely things!'
Well, so far she's got to first bass...

Chopin — let's just call him Fred —
Eloped with George Sand to the Med.
        (I hasten to mensh
        That George S. was a wench,
In case some dear reader's misled...)

A cruising musician called Tarr
Got stranded in far Panama:
'I had a great Christhmus,'
He said, 'on the isthmus,
Just getting well-sthloshed in a bar!'

Said a lumberjack out in Johore:
'Ugh! Chopping down trees is a bore!'
So he switched his career
To music — I hear
He's a dab hand on musical saw…

Ricardo, a globe-trotting Roman,
Is quite an incredible showman;
He'll sing *Carolina*
In the Morning in China,
And then he'll play Rome in the gloamin'.

The trombone's antecedent, of course,
Was the sackbut, a word whose strange
source
I found in some book:
It's Old French for 'a hook
For pulling a man off a horse'...

There's nothing like music: I play
My records by night and by day;
   But I've made a decision
   To avoid *EUROVISION* —
It's *nothing* like music, I say!

There's an old Country singer called Rudy,
Who's never bad-tempered or moody;
   He'll greet you with: 'Hey,
   Pardner — whaddyou say!'
Or sometimes, just: 'Howdya-doody!'

Schubert's Unfinished Limerick

'A limerick writer, I'm not —
But I'll try!' said Franz Schubert: 'Mein Gott!
I haf the first line!
(Es gibt rather fine?):
"There voss and old man…"' *(dot, dot, dot)*